HISTORY'S GREATEST RIVALS

JOHN F. KENNEDY

Vs.

NIKITA KHRUSHCHEV

COLD WAR ADVERSARIES

Ellis Roxburgh

Gareth Stevens
PUBLISHING

Please visit our website, **www.garethstevens.com**. For a free color catalog of all our high-quality books, call toll-free 1-800-542-2595 or fax 1-877-542-2596.

Library of Congress Cataloging-in-Publication Data

Roxburgh, Ellis.
John F. Kennedy vs. Nikita Khrushchev / Ellis Roxburgh.
    pages cm. — (History's greatest rivals)
Includes index.
ISBN 978-1-4824-2223-8 (pbk.)
ISBN 978-1-4824-2224-5 (6 pack)
ISBN 978-1-4824-2221-4 (library binding)
1. Cold War—Juvenile literature. 2. World politics—1945-1989—Juvenile literature. 3. United States—Foreign relations—Soviet Union—Juvenile literature. 4. Soviet Union—Foreign relations—United States—Juvenile literature. 5. Cuban Missile crisis, 1962—Juvenile literature. 6. Kennedy, John F. (John Fitzgerald), 1917-1963—Juvenile literature. 7. Khrushchev, Nikita Sergeevich, 1894-1971—Juvenile literature. I. Title.
D843.R678 2015
327.7304709'046—dc23

2014024263

Published in 2015 by
Gareth Stevens Publishing
111 East 14th Street, Suite 349
New York, NY 10003

© 2015 Brown Bear Books Ltd

For Brown Bear Books Ltd:
Editorial Director: Lindsey Lowe
Managing Editor: Tim Cooke
Children's Publisher: Anne O'Daly
Design Manager: Keith Davis
Designer: Mary Walsh and Karen Perry
Picture Manager: Sophie Mortimer

Picture Credits Front Cover: Alamy: Everett Collection Historical left, ITAR-Tass Photo Agency right; Robert Hunt Library: background. Alamy: Everett Collection Historical 4, 42l, ITAR-Tass Photo Agency 5, 43r; Bundesarchiv: ifcr; Getty Images: Express Newspapers 11; John F. Kennedy Library: 10, 14, 19, 36; Library of Congress: 6; RIAN Archive: 23; Robert Hunt Library: ifcl, 7, 8, 9, 12, 18, 21, 24, 25, 27, 28, 29, 30, 31, 33, 37, 38, 39, 42/43, 45; Thinkstock: iStock 40; U.S. Department of Defense: 17, 22; U.S. National Archives: 13, 15, 20, 26, 32, 34, 35, 41; Yoichi R. Okamoto: 16.
Artistic Effects Shutterstock

Brown Bear Books has made every attempt to contact the copyright holder. If anyone has any information please contact licensing@brownbearbooks.co.uk

Manufactured in the United States of America
CPSIA compliance information: Batch #CW15GS. For further information contact Gareth Stevens, New York, New York at 1-800-542-2595.

CONTENTS

AT ODDS

KENNEDY Vs. KHRUSHCHEV

John Fitzgerald Kennedy (1917–1963) became US president in 1960. He was young and dynamic. He promised to lead the United States in its ideological struggle with the communist Soviet Union.

* Kennedy was born into a rich Bostonian family and had a privileged upbringing.

* He served in the US Navy in the Pacific in World War II (1939–1945).

* He entered politics after his older brother, Joe, was killed in the war.

* He served as a junior senator before he won the presidential election.

* He was the youngest person, and first Catholic, to become US president.

Nikita Sergeyevich Khrushchev (1894–1971) worked his way up through the ranks of the Soviet Communist Party. After the dictator Joseph Stalin died in 1953 he became party general secretary, the effective leader of the Soviet Union.

* **Khrushchev was born into a peasant family. He had little formal education and became a metal worker.**

* **He believed he owed everything to the Communist Party and wanted the world to become communist.**

* **In World War II, he acted as a go-between for Stalin and his generals.**

CONTEXT

John F. Kennedy and Nikita Khrushchev both came to power in the early 1960s. The United States and the Soviet Union were involved in a political stand-off known as the Cold War.

In World War II, the two superpower countries had fought with France, Britain, and others against Nazi Germany and its allies, or supporters. At the end of the war, Soviet armies occupied much of eastern Europe. But the Americans and the Soviets quickly clashed over how to deal with Germany after its defeat.

Clashing Ideas

The United States wanted to help rebuild Germany, which would help create a strong European economy. The Soviets wanted to punish Germany for starting the war. The Russian leader, Joseph Stalin (1878–1953), was determined that Russia would not be invaded again. He created a buffer zone of communist countries in Eastern Europe that would protect Russia. By 1949, all of

ESCALATION: Dwight D. Eisenhower became president in 1953. He increased the number of troops stationed in Europe.

VIETNAM: Communist-backed Nationalists in Vietnam defeated their French rulers in 1954.

Eastern Europe was communist except Yugoslavia. The new US president, Harry S. Truman (1884–1972), was strongly anticommunist. In 1947, he declared in the Truman Doctrine that America would help halt the spread of communism anywhere in the world. This set the tone for 40 years of tension between Russia and the United States.

" The Russians only understand one language: how many armies have you got? "

President Harry S. Truman, 1945

Berlin Airlift

After World War II, the Soviets occupied East Germany. The German capital, Berlin, was deep inside East Germany. The city was divided into four sectors controlled by the Americans, British, French, and Soviets. In 1948, the Western powers introduced a new currency in West Berlin. In response, Stalin cut off rail and road links through East Germany to the city.

The Allies reacted by flying in 1.5 million tons of supplies to stop West Berlin from starving. This "Berlin Airlift" lasted 318 days.

Growing Tensions

Tensions between the superpowers grew. In 1949, the United States joined the newly formed North Atlantic Treaty Organization (NATO). It was an alliance of countries that promised to defend each other from attack—meaning attack from the Soviet Union. The Soviets saw this as a provocation. Then, in 1950 the Soviets backed communist North Korea in its invasion of noncommunist South Korea. The Americans joined United Nations forces to fight against the aggression. They saw the invasion as

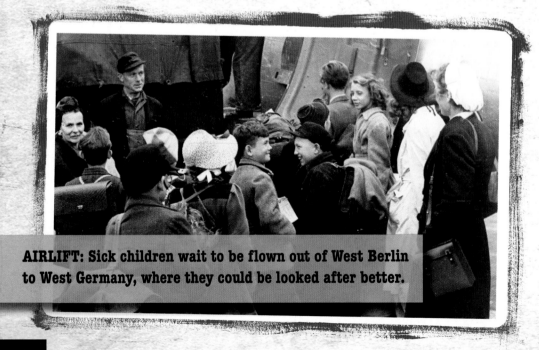

AIRLIFT: Sick children wait to be flown out of West Berlin to West Germany, where they could be looked after better.

RUINS: Berlin was left in ruins after World War II. In the Soviet sector, signs were written in German and also the Russian Cyrillic alphabet.

evidence of the "domino theory." This argued that if one country fell to communism, its neighbor became more likely to fall in turn. The war ended with the establishment of North and South Korea as separate nations.

New Leaders, Old Struggle

Truman's successor, Dwight D. Eisenhower, came to office in 1953. That same year Stalin died and was replaced by Nikita Khrushchev. In 1955 Khrushchev set up the Warsaw Pact, an alliance of communist countries to rival NATO. Eisenhower raised the number of NATO troops stationed in Germany. The Russian invasion of Hungary in 1956, after it tried to leave the Warsaw Pact, gave the United States a clear indication of what the Soviet Union would do to control its neighbors and further raised tensions between the two superpowers.

LINES ARE DRAWN

John F. Kennedy and Nikita Sergeyevich Khrushchev became the spokesmen for the political beliefs of their respective countries.

Joseph Stalin died in 1953. Nikita Khrushchev replaced him as First Secretary of the Communist Party of the Soviet Union. In 1956 he came to the world's attention with a speech in which he denounced Stalin. Previously, no one had dared to say anything negative about the previous leader. Now Khrushchev said Stalin had been a dictator who had committed many crimes against the Soviet people.

Despite this, Khrushchev remained a firm believer in Stalin's communism. He thought all property should belong to the state, and that the state should control people's lives. He believed that eventually the world

HOPEFUL: Many Americans saw Kennedy's youth and energy as a positive benefit.

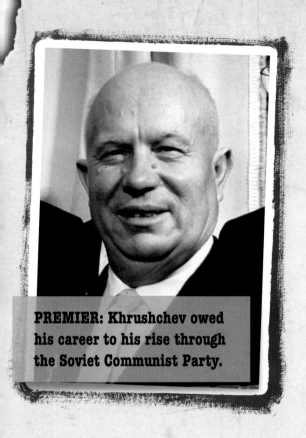

PREMIER: Khrushchev owed his career to his rise through the Soviet Communist Party.

would become communist. The United States was enjoying a consumer boom based on economic freedom— the very opposite of communist beliefs. Americans were nervous about the Soviet domination of Eastern Europe. The 1960 presidential election was dominated by the threat of communism. John F. Kennedy, at the time a young Democratic senator from Massachusetts, was elected on a promise to deal firmly with the communist threat.

First Meeting

By then, the two men had already met. As a senator, Kennedy attended an official tea party during Khrushchev's visit to the United States in September 1959. Khrushchev reportedly said to Kennedy, "I've heard a lot about you."

> **People say you have a great future ahead of you.**
>
> **Nikita Khrushchev to JFK, 1959**

JOHN F. KENNEDY

John F. Kennedy came from a wealthy and powerful Massachusetts family. They were used to being involved in national politics.

John Fitzgerald Kennedy was the second of the nine children of Rose and Joseph P. "Joe" Kennedy. Joe Kennedy was the son of Irish immigrants. He made a fortune through investments and served as the US ambassador to Britain. His children enjoyed a privileged upbringing in Boston, Massachusetts. After boarding school and Harvard University, JFK joined the US Navy in World War II.

Political Career Begins

When JFK's eldest brother, Joe, was killed in the war, their father persuaded John to take his place and run for Congress. After serving three terms, JFK was elected to the Senate in 1952. In the late 1950s, he decided he would run for president in 1960. He secured the Democratic Party nomination. The Texan senator Lyndon B. Johnson was his running mate.

HERO: Kennedy captained a torpedo boat in the Pacific in World War II.

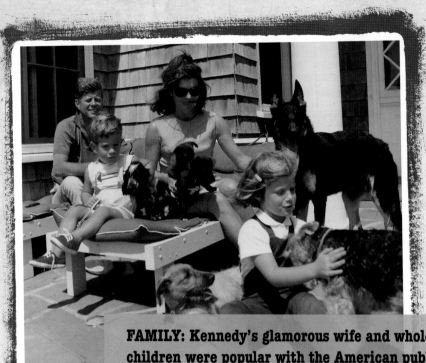

FAMILY: Kennedy's glamorous wife and wholesome children were popular with the American public.

They won a narrow victory over the Republican vice president, Richard M. Nixon. Kennedy was the youngest ever president at just 43, and was also the first Catholic president.

> ❝ Ask not what your country can do for you; ask what you can do for your country. ❞
>
> **John F. Kennedy inauguration speech, 1961**

Optimistic Future

With his beautiful young wife, Jackie, and two young children in the White House, JFK represented the new America: forward-looking and modern. For him, communism was a backward way of thinking. He saw the Soviet dominance of Eastern Europe as something that had to be stopped.

NIKITA KHRUSHCHEV

The Soviet premier's education and wartime experiences could hardly have been more different from those of his rival in the White House.

Nikita Sergeyevich Khrushchev was born into a peasant family in western Russia. He had little education. As a teenager, he became a metalworker. In 1917, communists led the Russian Revolution against the royal family. The following year, Khrushchev joined the communist Bolsheviks. Before the revolution, Khrushchev's opportunities had been limited. Afterward he was able to study as an engineer. This made him a great believer in communism as a way of giving everyone an opportunity. Over the next 30 years, Khrushchev worked his way up in the Communist Party, which was

ASSISTANT: Khrushchev worked closely with Soviet dictator Joseph Stalin but later denounced him.

VISIT: Khrushchev (second from right) and his wife (far left) attend a dinner with President and Mrs. Eisenhower in 1959.

dominated by Joseph Stalin. In 1939, he became a member of the Politburo, the party's ruling committee. He worked closely with Stalin during World War II. Following Stalin's death in 1953, Khrushchev became the First Secretary of the party. He was now the most powerful man in the Soviet Union.

> **We will not bury you with a shovel. Your own working class will bury you.**
>
> **Nikita Khrushchev**

Communist Champion

In order to prove that communism could work as well as capitalism, Khrushchev ordered ambitious food programs. Some failed, such as planting corn where it would not grow. In 1956, Khrushchev denounced Stalin as a cruel dictator. That led to him falling out with Chairman Mao Zedong, the leader of communist China and a former ally of Stalin.

KENNEDY'S CABINET

When Kennedy took office in January 1961, he gathered a group of White House and National Security Council advisors around him.

Kennedy wanted these men to reflect a new mood of optimism and idealism. He called them the "brightest and the best." They would offer a range of ways to respond to the different challenges posed by the Soviet Union and the Cold War. His team included "Hawks," who wanted to stand up to the Soviets and threaten force if necessary, and "Doves," who preferred compromise and negotiation.

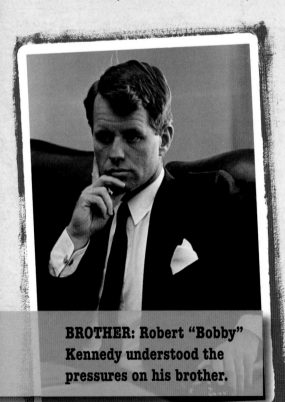

Hawks and Doves

Many of the most powerful men in the administration were Doves. They included Secretary of Defense Robert S. McNamara,

BROTHER: Robert "Bobby" Kennedy understood the pressures on his brother.

> **" We have the power to make this the best generation of mankind in the history of the world—or make it the last. "**
>
> **John F. Kennedy, 1963**

DOVE: Robert McNamara was one of the most important voices in favor of compromise and peace.

who had just become president of Ford Motor Cars when he joined the Cabinet. He advised Kennedy to abandon Eisenhower's policy of "massive retaliation" in response to a Soviet threat. Secretary of State Dean Rusk was another influential Dove.

Controversial Appointment

The most controversial appointment in Kennedy's cabinet was his closest ally, his younger brother, Robert. Outside the Cabinet, Kennedy had unlikely allies in former presidents and the Republicans, who supported his fight against communism. The British prime minister, Harold Macmillan, was also a great help. At times of great tension, the two men spoke on the telephone every day.

SOVIET ALLIES

Khrushchev had the backing of the Communist Party in the Soviet Union. He also made crucial alliances with other communist leaders.

ENEMY: China's Mao Zedong disliked Khrushchev's aims.

As First Secretary of the Communist Party, Khrushchev was a virtual dictator. He had the last say on everything within the Soviet Union. But he was also part of a ruling group called the Politburo. He could be overthrown by powerful enemies within the group. As long as he maintained a powerful presence on the world's stage, however, Khrushchev had nothing to fear from his closest associates.

Diplomatic Allies

Khrushchev and the Soviet Communist Party were both committed to spreading communism throughout the world. Khrushchev's closest allies in this were all skilled international diplomats. They included his special assistant for international affairs, Oleg Troyanovsky, who grew up in Washington, DC, and spoke perfect English. The Soviet ambassador to the United States, Anatoly Dobrynin, and Foreign Minister Andrei Gromyko both understood international affairs well.

DIPLOMACY: President Kennedy meets the Soviet foreign minister Andrei Gromyko.

Communist China

China was the world's largest communist state, under Chairman Mao Zedong. China and the Soviet Union were close allies, but Mao and Khrushchev fell out in the early 1960s. The Chinese were unhappy that the Soviets did not support their disputes with Taiwan and India. Mao disliked Khrushchev's attempts to make alliances with the West. He called the Soviet leader a "psalm-singing buffoon." Khrushchev's main international ally turned out to be Fidel Castro, the leader of the revolution in Cuba, America's near neighbor.

> " He acted how an immoral gangster would act, and not as a statesman. "
>
> **Kennedy on Khrushchev**

FIRST CLASHES

» KHRUSHCHEV AND EISENHOWER

Kennedy was not the first US president to meet Khrushchev. In September 1959 Eisenhower invited the Soviet leader to the United States.

The 2-week visit was meant to improve relations between the two countries. Soviet success in space technology had led to US fears that a "missile gap" was opening between the two powers. Meanwhile, there were growing concerns about the situation in Germany. In 1956, when the Hungarian leader had announced that Hungary would leave the Warsaw Pact, Soviet tanks rolled into the Hungarian capital, Budapest, to enforce Soviet rule. The Americans were concerned that something similar might happen in Germany.

FARMING: Khrushchev visits an Iowa dairy farm during his trip to the United States in 1959.

FIRST: In April 1961, Soviet cosmonaut Yuri Gagarin became the first man in space.

Short-Lived Optimism

Khrushchev's visit included dining with Marilyn Monroe and other movie stars in Hollywood. There was also a 2-day summit meeting with Eisenhower at Camp David, the president's official retreat. The summit was intended to iron out differences and to halt any buildup of nuclear weapons. The optimism of the summit was short-lived, however. Kennedy would inherit a situation of raised tensions with the Soviets.

> **The question of disarmament is the most important one facing the world today.**
>
> Joint communiqué, Camp David, September 1959

U-2 INCIDENT

In 1960, Eisenhower and Khrushchev were due to meet in Paris. That month, however, a US spy plane was shot down in Soviet airspace.

HIGH-FLIER: The U-2 was wrongly thought to be immune to Soviet missiles and airplanes.

The United States was flying secret missions to discover the extent of Soviet nuclear weaponry. Eisenhower had suggested that both sides be allowed to fly in the other's airspace to check for nuclear sites, but Khrushchev had rejected the idea.

Spies in the Skies

However, the US Air Force began to use the U-2 reconnaissance aircraft as a spy plane to photograph Soviet installations. It flew at high altitudes that Soviet missiles and planes could not reach. On May 1, 1960, an American U-2 spy plane was shot down in Soviet

WRECKAGE: Soviet citizens examine the wreck of the plane, which was put on public display.

airspace. The pilot, Gary Powers, bailed out and was captured. The Americans denied spying and invented an elaborate cover-up story. When the Soviets produced photographs Powers had taken of military installations, however, the US could not deny it anymore. The evidence was highly embarrassing. The Soviets put Powers on trial for spying and sentenced him to 3 years in prison and 7 years' hard labor.

> **We have parts of the plane, and we also have the pilot, who is quite alive and kicking.**
>
> **Nikita Khrushchev, May 1960**

Stormy Summit

Two weeks later, Khrushchev and Eisenhower flew to Paris for the summit. Khrushchev demanded that Eisenhower apologize. The president refused, and the Soviet leader stormed out. The result was far reaching.

CRISIS IN BERLIN

The failed Paris summit had far-reaching consequences. The question of what to do about post-war Berlin became more urgent.

Berlin had been divided into four sectors at the end of World War II. The west of the city was under US, British, and French control. The Soviets controlled both East Berlin and the surrounding communist state, the German Democratic Republic, or East Germany.

Ongoing Concern

The existence of West Berlin deep inside communist East Germany was a concern for both sides. As early as 1948, Stalin had blocked off road and rail access to the city. The Berlin Airlift flew in supplies to

ACHTUNG!
Sie verlassen jetzt
WEST-BERLIN

DIVIDED: To begin with, it was relatively easy to cross between West and East Berlin.

BARRIER: The Soviets blocked off access between West and East Berlin in 1961.

keep West Berlin going. Many Eastern Europeans disliked communist rule, and during the 1950s thousands of people fled to the West. Estimates suggest as many as 3.5 million people passed through the city to West Berlin.

> **What happens to Berlin, happens to Germany; what happens to Germany, happens to Europe.**
>
> **Vyacheslav Molotov, Soviet foreign minister, 1948**

Ideological Battleground

A decade after the end of World War II, Berlin remained a thorn in the side of the Soviets. In November 1958, Khrushchev demanded that the Western powers leave Berlin within 6 months. Eisenhower refused, and Berlin became an ideological battleground. The tensions over Berlin remained unresolved when President Kennedy took office in January 1961.

FACE TO FACE

Kennedy and Khrushchev met only twice. On June 4, 1961, they held a face-to-face meeting in Vienna, the capital of Austria.

When Khrushchev had met President Eisenhower in 1959, the talks had been bad tempered. In contrast, the meeting in Vienna was quite friendly. But there were serious issues to discuss. Both the United States and the Soviet Union governed sectors of Berlin. The former German capital was deep inside communist East Germany.

Power Battle

Khrushchev believed that he was senior to Kennedy and more experienced. He decided to try and take advantage. He threatened to sign a treaty with East Germany that would give East Germany

WATCHFUL: Kennedy watches Khrushchev during a joint press conference.

FAREWELL: Kennedy and Khrushchev leave at the end of the summit.

control over the air and road routes to Berlin. That would make it possible for Berlin to be cut off. Kennedy insisted that the routes to Berlin had to remain open. Khrushchev demanded that the Allies should leave Berlin. He said he would sign the agreement anyway. Kennedy said "Then, Mr. Chairman, there will be war."

> **Force will be met by force. If the United States wants war, that's its problem.**
>
> **Nikita Khrushchev, 1961**

Who Won?

To begin with, the Americans thought the meeting had gone well for Kennedy. He had stood up to Khrushchev. But Kennedy had talked a lot about "West Berlin." Khrushchev decided that meant he was free to do what he wanted in East Berlin, even to close the borders. Eventually, Khrushchev would get his way—and Kennedy would remember the Vienna summit as the worst day of his life.

THE WALL GOES UP

On August 13, 1961, Berliners found their city divided by a barrier that would become a symbol of the Cold War: the Berlin Wall.

Khrushchev's demand that the Americans leave Berlin put him and Kennedy in a difficult position. Kennedy told Americans on August 3, 1961, that more US troops would be sent to Europe, and that there might be a nuclear attack. Although he was not ready to go to war over Berlin, he wanted Khrushchev to believe he would.

DIVIDE: A family looks on as the wall goes up and divides them from their neighbors.

The Wall Goes Up

In early August, Khrushchev gave approval for the building of a barricade between East and West Berlin. In the 24 hours after Kennedy's speech to his fellow Americans more than 3,000 East Berliners had fled to the West. Khrushchev believed he had to act.

A Free Hand

Khrushchev suggested the barrier be built from barbed wire to see how the Allies reacted. When they did not react, he went ahead with constructing a wall from concrete. But it was a diplomatic disaster for Khrushchev. It symbolized everything that was wrong with communism. Kennedy had won a victory of sorts. He had backed down, but he had avoided a war.

WINDOW: A Berliner looks out of an apartment block at the wall which has been built outside.

> **❝** It's not a very nice solution, but a Wall is... a lot better than a war. **❞**

John F. Kennedy, 1961

CUBAN MISSILE CRISIS

For 7 days in October 1962 the world held its breath. The Soviet Union and the United States were on the brink of a nuclear war.

Cuba lies just 90 miles (150 km) off the coast of Florida. In 1959, Fidel Castro led a rebellion on the island to overthrow the corrupt dictator Fulgencio Batista. The United States had supported Batista and had many business interests in Cuba. Castro seized all the US assets. In return, the United States stopped importing Cuban sugar, which was Cuba's main source of income. The Soviet Union stepped in and bought the sugar. Castro was not a communist, but he now found his country dependent on communist support.

BLOCKADE: A US Navy plane flies above ships blockading Cuba.

MRBM LAUNCH SITE 2
SAN CRISTOBAL
1 NOVEMBER 1962

FUEL TRAILERS

MISSILE READY TENT

FORMER LAUNCH POSITIONS

FORMER LOCATION OF MISSILE READY TENTS

INTELLIGENCE: This picture of a missile base on Cuba was taken at the end of the crisis.

Bay of Pigs Invasion

The US Central Intelligence Agency (CIA) planned to strike back against Castro by training, arming, and funding anti-Castro Cubans in the United States. In April 1961, after President Kennedy had inherited the plan from President Eisenhower, the CIA transported 1,300 Cuban exiles to the Bay of Pigs in Cuba. They planned to spark an uprising to overthrow Castro. Instead, the invasion was to be a disaster.

Missile Crisis

On October 14, 1962, US spy planes photographed Russian-built missiles being assembled at bases on Cuba. That brought almost every US city within range of a Soviet nuclear attack. When Kennedy was told about this 2 days later, he faced a dilemma. If he invaded Cuba, there might be a nuclear war—but he dare not let the missiles be built. He decided the best way to stop this was to prevent the parts reaching the Cuban bases. He announced a naval blockade to prevent ships sailing to Cuba. Khrushchev said this would be an act of war.

Secret Meetings

On October 22, 1962, Kennedy went on US TV to explain to Americans the seriousness of the situation. He and his advisors had decided a line of ships would form a "quarantine" to halt Soviet

SIGNATURE: Kennedy signs the order bringing the blockade of Cuba into effect.

" We and you ought not now to pull on the ends of the rope in which you have tied the knot of war. "

Khrushchev's letter to Kennedy, October 1962

ALLY: Khrushchev was close allies with Fidel Castro, president of Cuba, before and after the Missile Crisis.

ships headed to Cuba. In secret, however, the Americans also started talking to the Soviets about closing US missile bases in Turkey.

The World Waits

As the world waited, Khrushchev took the first step away from conflict. The Russian ships turned back. Khrushchev sent a telegram to Kennedy offering to dismantle the Cuban bases if the Americans lifted the blockade. A second telegram demanded the dismantling of the US Turkish bases. In a show of strength, a US spy plane was shot down. Kennedy ignored this, however. He agreed publicly to Khrushchev's first telegram and secretly to the second. The world congratulated Kennedy for having stood up to communism (no one knew about the secret Turkish deal until much later). Meanwhile, Khrushchev had lost face; China even broke off relations with Russia.

SOUTHEAST ASIA

Southeast Asia was far from both the United States and the Soviet Union. But it became a key battleground in the Cold War.

In 1954, the French withdrew from their Southeast Asian colony of Indochina, which became Vietnam, Laos, and Cambodia. Laos fell under Soviet influence and was in danger of becoming communist. President Eisenhower had committed millions of dollars to prevent this, but Kennedy moved cautiously. He refused to send troops to Laos. Instead he decided to negotiate a settlement with the Soviets. He and Khrushchev went to Geneva in July 1962 to announce Laos's neutrality, although they did not meet one-on-one.

VIETNAM: US troops set out on a patrol in Vietnam after arriving in Asia in 1963.

DESTRUCTION: A US Boeing B-52 rains bombs on North Vietnam in 1964.

Trouble in Vietnam

After the French left Vietnam in 1954, the country split in two. Communists controlled North Vietnam and wanted to take control of South Vietnam. In 1961, Kennedy decided to increase the number of US troops in South Vietnam from 500 to 16,000. Khrushchev wanted the whole of Vietnam to become communist, but he was worried about provoking war with the United States.

A Slow Defeat

Neither Khrushchev nor Kennedy was in power when the Vietnam War reached its peak in the mid-1960s. The fight against communism in Southeast Asia eventually ended in a humiliating defeat for the United States.

> " If you want to, go ahead and fight in the jungles of Vietnam, but eventually the Americans will have to quit. "
>
> Nikita Khrushchev, 1963

DEATH OF KENNEDY

By fall 1963, although tensions were building in Vietnam, Kennedy and Khrushchev had avoided war in Cuba and Berlin.

OPEN TARGET: President and Jackie Kennedy drove through Dallas in an open car like this one.

The two leaders had developed a good understanding. In October 1963 Khrushchev had written again to Kennedy to tell him that they must find a solution to conflict. A Limited Test Ban Treaty on nuclear development would be the first step. But the relationship between the two men ended suddenly on November 22, 1963. President Kennedy was shot dead in Dallas, Texas.

HEADLINES: A newspaper carries a photo of Lyndon B. Johnson being sworn in as president.

Soviet Plot?

In the United States, suspicion fell immediately on the Soviet Union. The man who was arrested as the assassin, Lee Harvey Oswald, had lived in the Soviet Union. But Oswald was murdered before he could stand trial. New suspects emerged, including the Cubans and organized crime gangs in the United States. In fact, Khrushchev had burst into tears when he was told of Kennedy's death. He knew that the new president, Lyndon B. Johnson, was fiercely anti-communist. He feared that the two superpowers were about to return to the darkest days of the Cold War.

> ❝ You were allied in a determination that the world should not be blown up. ❞

Jackie Kennedy to Khrushchev, 1963

KHRUSHCHEV OUT

With Kennedy's death, Khrushchev lost his one-time rival and ally. He now faced a new president who was a known anti-communist.

The assassination of Kennedy coincided with a difficult time in the Soviet Union. Drought across the country had wiped out the wheat crops, and fall 1963 produced a disastrous harvest. Khrushchev's solution was to produce more chemical fertilizers, but that was a long-term solution. The Soviet Union might soon be starving. Instead, Khrushchev was forced to turn to his Cold War enemy. The Soviet Union bought wheat from the United States. However, this weakened Khrushchev's position with his colleagues in the Politburo.

Downfall
Khrushchev had become unpopular with powerful

SUCCESSOR: Leonid Brezhnev led a plot because he feared Khrushchev had made the Soviet Union less stable.

BERLIN: Under Brezhnev the German capital remained divided.

communists such as Leonid Brezhnev. They disliked the power of his personality, the failure of his agricultural policies, and his sudden decisions. They were angry that he had fallen out with China. The purchase of US wheat was the final blow. And with the death of Kennedy, Khrushchev could no longer claim that the relationship he had built with the US president was a reason to stay in office. Some of Khrushchev's closest allies began to plot against him. On October 13, 1964, he was told that his time as First Secretary of the Communist Party was over. He was succeeded by Leonid Brezhnev.

> " I'm old and tired. Let them cope by themselves. I've done the main thing. "
>
> **Nikita Khrushchev, 1964**

AFTERMATH

Kennedy and Khrushchev's rivalry spanned almost 4 years. Despite near disaster, they had avoided nuclear war.

The Limited Test Ban Treaty (LTBT), intended to limit the production of nuclear weapons, was signed in October 1963. It limited the testing of nuclear weapons, apart from underwater tests. After the ban was signed, Khrushchev wrote to Kennedy urging that they must find a way to maintain peace between the two nations. Kennedy agreed, but his reply was not sent. A month later he was dead.

SYMBOL: The Berlin Wall remained a highly visible symbol of the Cold War until 1989.

SUMMIT: President Johnson (right) and Soviet premier Alexei Kosygin hold arms talks in June 1967.

End of the Cold War

In the later 1960s and 1970s, there were more bans limiting arms development. There were also further flashpoints between East and West—but never again on the scale of the Cuban Missile Crisis. In the end, however, the threat of nuclear war passed because of changes in the Soviet Union. In 1989 and 1990 the communist Eastern bloc collapsed in a series of popular uprisings and political changes. The Soviet Union broke up. The countries of Eastern Europe became independent democracies. If the Cold War had a victor, it was the United States and its allies in the free world.

> **It is an ironic but accurate fact that the two strongest powers are the two in the most danger of devastation.**
>
> **John F. Kennedy, 1963**

JUDGMENT

KENNEDY Vs. KHRUSHCHEV

Kennedy's death robbed the world of a dynamic young leader. The shock of his assassination still hangs over US politics. His name remains one of the best remembered of all politicians.

* JFK did not manage to resolve tensions over Berlin. The city remained divided until the Wall was torn down in 1989.

* Kennedy's stand during the Cuban Missile Crisis brought the world dangerously close to nuclear war, but was ultimately successful.

* Kennedy saw nuclear weapons as the biggest danger facing the world. His attempts to limit them, however, were supported by Khrushchev.

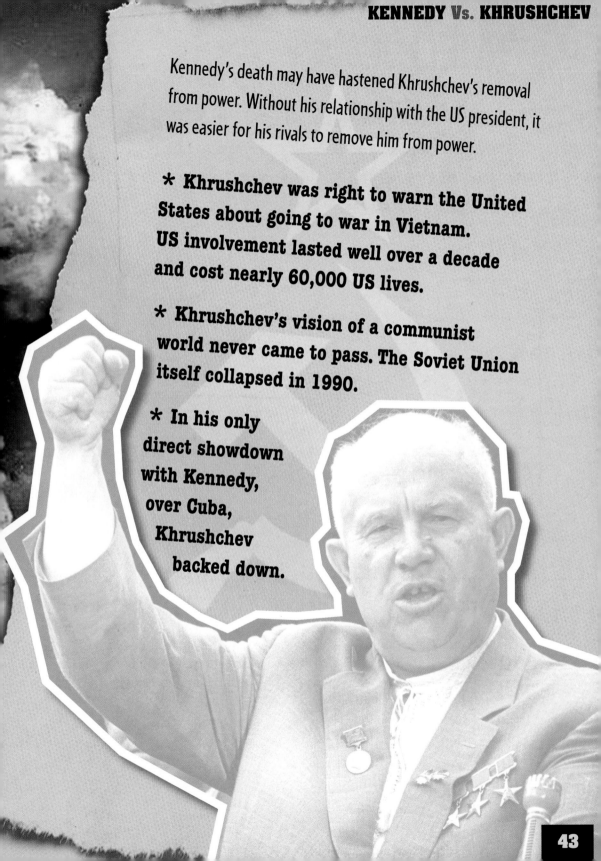

Kennedy's death may have hastened Khrushchev's removal from power. Without his relationship with the US president, it was easier for his rivals to remove him from power.

✴ **Khrushchev was right to warn the United States about going to war in Vietnam. US involvement lasted well over a decade and cost nearly 60,000 US lives.**

✴ **Khrushchev's vision of a communist world never came to pass. The Soviet Union itself collapsed in 1990.**

✴ **In his only direct showdown with Kennedy, over Cuba, Khrushchev backed down.**

TIMELINE

The direct rivalry between Kennedy and Khrushchev lasted for less than 3 years, but it was part of the far longer ideological rivalry known as the Cold War.

Divided Europe
At the end of World War II, Soviet troops occupy eastern Europe. Berlin, inside East Germany, is divided among the Soviet Union, the United States, Britain, and France.

A New Leader
Upon the death of Stalin, Nikita Khrushchev becomes leader of the Soviet Union. Later in the year he forms the Warsaw Pact.

Spy Plane
In May, a US U-2 spy plane is shot down over the Soviet Union, causing great embarrassment to the US government.

1945   **1948**   **1953** **1959**   **1959** **1961**

Berlin Airlift
The Soviet Union blocks all land access to Berlin. The Western powers use aircraft to fly in supplies.

US Visit
Khrushchev visits the United States at the invitation of President Dwight D. Eisenhower.

New President
In January, John F. Kennedy is inaugurated as US president.

Failed Invasion
In April, a US-backed invasion of Cuba to topple Fidel Castro ends in failure.

Missile Crisis
In October, Kennedy forces Khrushchev to dismantle Soviet missile bases being built on Cuba; for a time, the danger of nuclear war seems very real.

Assassination
In November, Kennedy is shot dead by an assassin in Dallas, Texas; Khrushchev cries when he is told the news.

1961   **1962** **1963**   **1964**

Vienna Summit
In June, Kennedy and Khrushchev meet in Vienna, Austria, to discuss Berlin; 2 months later, Khrushchev orders the construction of the Berlin Wall.

Test Ban Treaty
In October, Kennedy and Khrushchev agree to limit testing of nuclear weapons; both men intend to further reduce the nuclear arms race.

Forced Out
In October, Khrushchev's enemies in the Communist Party force him out of his position; he is replaced by Leonid Brezhnev.

GLOSSARY

alliance An association of countries or organizations in which the members benefit one another.

allies Countries that work together to achieve a particular goal.

assassination A murder committed for political or ideological reasons.

bloc A group of countries that share similar interests and often work together.

blockade The act of sealing off a place so that no goods or people can enter or leave.

Bolsheviks A group who came to control the Russian Communist Party.

buffer zone A neutral area that separates hostile neighbors.

capitalism A political system based on economic and personal freedom.

communism A political system that promotes the limiting of personal property and state control of the economy.

dictator A ruler who has complete control over a country.

Doves A name given to people who take a peaceful or diplomatic approach to foreign affairs.

fertilizer A chemical that provides nutrients to soil to help crops grow.

Hawks A name given to people who take an aggressive or militaristic attitude toward foreign affairs.

ideological Describes an attitude based on someone's political, religious, or moral beliefs.

nuclear weapons Bombs that generate tremendous explosive power by a chemical chain reaction.

Politburo In a communist party, the committee that decides what policies to follow.

quarantine Keeping someone in isolation to prevent him or her spreading an infectious disease.

retaliation An attack on someone in response to an attack they have made.

FOR FURTHER INFORMATION

Books

Brownell, Richard. *The Cold War* (American History). Lucent Books, 2008.

Harper, Judith E. *John F. Kennedy* (Presidents of the U.S.A.). The Child's World, Inc. 2014.

Harrison, Paul. *Why Did the Cold War Happen?* (Moments in History). Gareth Stevens Publishing, 2010.

McNeese, Tim. *The Cold War and Postwar America 1946–1963* (Discovering U.S. History). Chelsea House Publishers, 2010.

Samuels, Charlie. *The Cuban Missile Crisis* (Turning Points in US Military History). Gareth Stevens Publishing, 2014.

Zuchora-Walske, Christine. *The Berlin Wall* (Essential Events). Abdo Publishing Company, 2014.

Websites

www.historylearningsite.co.uk/coldwar.htm
A site that tells the story of the Cold War in detail, including the Kennedy–Khrushchev period.

www.nationalarchives.gov.uk/education/coldwar/
A students' site from the UK National Archives, with a timeline, glossary, and analysis of major events.

www.history.com/topics/cold-war
Videos and facts about the Cold War from History.com.

www.jfklibrary.org/JFK/JFK-in-History/Cuban-Missile-Crisis.aspx
Special exhibit about the Cuban Missile Crisis from the John F. Kennedy President Library, with behind-the-scenes photographs.

INDEX